THE FIVE MARKS OF A MAN
TACTICAL
GUIDE

THE FIVE MARKS OF A MAN
TACTICAL
GUIDE

BRIAN TOME

BakerBooks

a division of Baker Publishing Group
Grand Rapids, Michigan

© 2023 by Brian Tome

Published by Baker Books
a division of Baker Publishing Group
Grand Rapids, Michigan
www.bakerbooks.com

Printed in the United States of America

ISBN 978-1-5409-0313-6 (paper)
ISBN 978-1-4934-4336-9 (ebook)

Published in association with The Bindery Agency, LLC, www.TheBinderyAgency.com.

Baker Publishing Group publications use paper produced from sustainable forestry practices and post-consumer waste whenever possible.

23   24   25   26   27   28   29   7   6   5   4   3   2   1

CONTENTS

WHAT MAKES A MAN?

BOYS ARE BORN.
MEN ARE MADE.

Something in our world has gone wrong when it comes to making men, and it seems to be a recent development.

Throughout history, men sat around the campfire to relive the day's hunt and bond with each other. Today's isolated male has no such option and no one to turn to. When we do connect, culture cracks jokes that we are on a "man date" and must be having a "bromance"— things that would never be said about women or a couple of five-year-olds in a sandbox.

Throughout history, men pooped in the woods like God intended. Today's sheltered American male doesn't know how to do such a thing without soiling his whitey tighties.

Throughout history, every male slept under the stars without electricity. Today's digitized male is intimidated by the sounds of nightfall.

Throughout history, men had a sense of the Divine. Some men took it even further and dared to walk with God. Today's male can't look away from his devices long enough to experience anything transcendent.

How did we get here? You could point the finger at any number of things, but I'm not interested in blame-shifting. Men don't do that. Instead, they see a problem and they fix it.

WHAT WE'RE MISSING, WHAT WE NEED, IS INITIATION.

Throughout the bulk of human history, boys were initiated into manhood. A boy couldn't become a man until he passed through this process—no matter how old, successful, or important (he thought) he was.

For some men, initiation meant going to the mountain and being circumcised. For others, it meant completing a difficult task or being apprenticed in the family trade. For my own son, it was a challenging motorcycle trip out West. Once initiated, going back to boyhood was no longer an option.

There were no participation trophies on the path to manhood, and not everyone made it through the gauntlet. But those who did were changed. They left boyhood behind, permanently.

Our Peter-Pan-perpetual-boyhood lifestyle is killing us. In America, men have a life expectancy five years less than females,[1] commit suicide at four times the rate of women,[2] and are two times as likely to have alcohol-related incidents and death.[3]

We don't have to accept the state of things. There is another way, an ancient and primal path, and I intend to walk it with you.

While initiation rites varied widely between cultures, there were a few commonalities:

A GUIDE

Boys can't find their way to manhood on their own. They've always been instructed and guided by a man who's walked the path before them.

A CHALLENGE

You didn't become a man by pouring a bowl of cereal in the morning. You had to do, or endure, something incredibly challenging.

A CEREMONY

The move to manhood was marked by a sacred moment, often with the initiated man being given a new name, identity, and role in society.

What follows in these pages is a tactical and practical guide for taking the path to authentic manhood. This can be your initiation, once and for all.

It doesn't matter how old you are or what boyish mistakes you've made in the past. It's never too late to embrace the ancient path to manhood. Men are defined by the choices they make, and the choice to dig in here can make all the difference.

In a sense, I will be your guide through this initiation. But you shouldn't do this alone. You will get infinitely more from this experience if you engage it with other men, whether it's a group of ten guys, a father-son combo, or anything in between. Bonus points if you invite someone older and wiser, a father figure, to come along with you.

From there, you'll find plenty of challenges in these pages to push you down the primal path of initiation. You will have to endure, push yourself, and get uncomfortable—but that's the point.

And at the end, I've included some ideas for marking this sacred moment in your life by holding your own initiation ceremony.

A guide, a challenge, and a ceremony. You have all the components you need for an initiation.

You were born a boy, but you're here, right now, to be made into a man. It's no accident you picked up this book. You are in the right place, and I believe in you.

READY FOR THE PATH TO MANHOOD?

LET'S GET TO IT.

ORIENTATION

The object you're holding in your hands has pages, binding, and a spine, but don't you dare think of it as a book. This is a tool—a masculine, tactile, participatory growth instrument.

That's a lot of words to say something simple: this ~~book~~ tool is meant to be used. If you're doing this thing right, it should get beat up. A pristine hammer means you've never driven a nail. We've got enough thinkers in the world. This experience is designed to make doers.

This guide works best as a companion to my book *The Five Marks of a Man*. This won't rehash everything in there. Instead, it will push you to act on it.

TO GET THE MOST OUT OF THIS EXPERIENCE

- Read *The Five Marks of a Man* either before or in tandem with this tactical guide.

- Engage every step, even the difficult ones.

- Do this with some other guys. You will learn more along the way.

- You could plow through this material in one sitting, but you shouldn't. Take your time, engage the journey with others, and allow each mark to settle and take root in your life.

TIME TO MOVE

This isn't your grandma's small group study, because you aren't looking to become a grandma. You're being initiated into manhood, and that's never happened by filling in blanks on a page.

This tool takes each mark, breaking it down into four sections:

LEARN

A short thought to get us all in the right mind space about that mark. Need more? Read the full-length book.

MOVE

Challenges designed to work each mark into your everyday life. Some are easy, some are hard. Don't be a wuss—push yourself.

TALK

Questions to mine for the gold. You can consider them alone, but these are best discussed with other guys.

PRAY

Close up shop by getting some quality time with your Father. Don't skip this one. Too many of us only pray for the difficulties that we face or for the pains of others who are in the hospital. Those are good and important prayers. But a man needs to learn to pray about other things that lead to a better life. And he needs to do it alongside others.

You're capable of coming up with your own way to move through this journey, but it could look like this:

ON YOUR OWN

1. Start by reading the **LEARN** section to get up to speed.

2. Read through all the **MOVE** challenges. Complete them before your group meets. How many should you do? As many as it takes to push you into uncomfortable territory. You don't build muscle any other way.

WITH YOUR GROUP

3. Get the guys together and work through the **TALK** questions. Start with the warm-up questions, letting each person answer just one. Then move to the group talking points, spending most of your time there. Be real, honest, and vulnerable.

4. Close out the mark by finishing the **PRAY** section as a group. Share what you've learned, what's next, and how your group can support you.

That's enough preamble for now. It's time to get on the path to manhood and start moving.

WELCOME TO YOUR INITIATION. LET'S GO.

MEN HAVE A VISION

MARK ONE

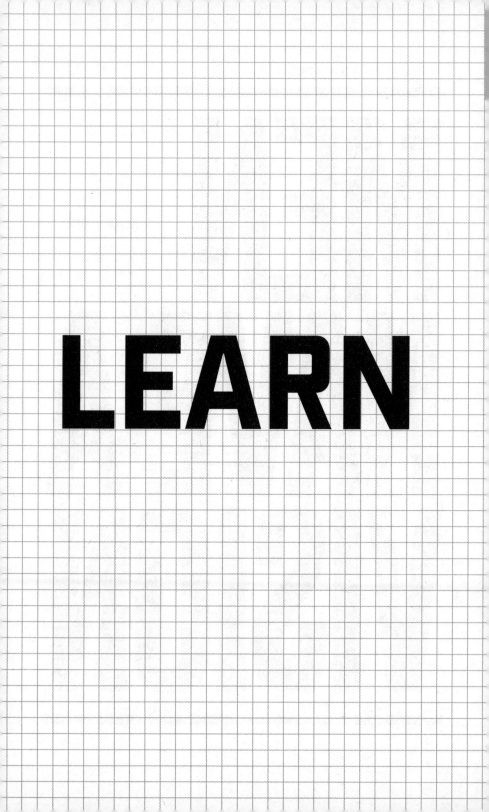

Boys love phrases like carpe diem and YOLO. It gives them a culturally acceptable excuse to be shallow and selfish.

Boys wake up and immediately start looking for what is going to make today a great day, with no thought about what that means for tomorrow.

MEN, ON THE OTHER HAND, HAVE VISION.

They can see beyond what's right in front of them to a meaningful finish line well in the distance. With their eyes fixed on "what could be," they take steps toward it today. And tomorrow. And the next day.

Saving for retirement. Beginning a workout routine. Asking a woman out in hopes of finding a life partner. Applying for a promotion. Saving up for a dream vacation. Reinstituting a date night with their wife. Raising kids. Vision requires movement now for a payoff later—and that's why boys don't do it.

Men have a vision, and they never age out of needing one to drive them forward.

One of the patriarchs of the Bible is a man named Abraham. Throughout Scripture, he's called "God's friend." Why? He had a vision that compelled him to move.

His story begins when he's seventy-five years old, living a well-established and prosperous life in a place called Haran. Then God shows up and throws a huge wrench into everything.

God actually asks this old man to uproot everything— his family, servants, flocks, and all his possessions—and move to a land he's never laid eyes on before.

How many old men do you know looking to completely upend their life? Crazier still, Abraham does it.

Even as all his friends are moving to Florida and watching *The Price Is Right* on repeat, Abraham has a vision that looks past the discomfort of now in order to focus on the blessings of later.

Be wary of people who poo-poo on getting more. Yes, contentment is a virtue and we all need more of it—but passivity is not. Abraham sets one foot in front of the other on a journey of five-hundred-plus miles because he wants more for his life.

He wants to be blessed by God. He wants a child. He wants to become a great nation and a blessing to the whole world.

Those are the promises God makes to Abraham, if the old man will just follow him. So he packs up his bags and gets to walking.

Vision doesn't bank on immediacy. It's a slow burn of some twenty-five years before Abraham begins to see the promises of God take place. But his vision for what could be keeps him moving. It's the same with you.

Every man has this in common: there's the place where we are right now, and the vision we have for the future. What lies between here and there is difficulty, perseverance, and time. Boys don't have the pain tolerance nor the patience necessary to make that trek. Men do.

What are you working on today that will pay off in twenty-five years? Do you have a slow burn? Are you chasing anything more profound than an easy day today?

MEN HAVE A VISION. IT'S TIME TO GET MOVING ON YOURS.

MOVE

PERSONAL CHALLENGES

CHALLENGE ONE: VISION QUEST

You don't have to be a Little Leaguer to know the cardinal rule of baseball: keep your eye on the ball.

Vision means putting your eyes and your body toward the finish line you're trying to cross. It means no matter what distractions come your way, you keep your eyes on the goal.

Test your vision by choosing one of the options below. *Remember, this isn't a book. It's a tool.*

☐ *Go outside and throw this guide as far as you can. Yes, right now. Then do it again. Repeat until you get some stains on the cover.*

☐ *Climb to the highest point you can access (A deer stand? A tree house? A mountainside?) and throw this guide from the top. Go get it.*

☐ *Put this guide on top of your car. Drive a few blocks. When you notice it's gone, go back and find it.*

☐ *Find some woods or a field. Throw this book into the undergrowth. Go find it.*

☐ *Take your dog outside and play fetch. Use this guide as your Frisbee.*

Lost the guide, then found it again? You've proven you have vision. Dig in more by answering these questions.

1

Sticking with a vision can get messy. Did you have a hard time throwing your book? Was there a part of you that wanted to keep it clean and pristine?

2

What roadblocks did you face when it came to recovering your book? Are there any lessons there that can carry over to chasing more meaningful visions?

3

"Get the book back" was a simple vision. When it comes to vision, simple is easier to chase and achieve. What things tend to complicate or cloud your vision? What can you do about them?

CHALLENGE TWO: HYPERFOCUS

The secret ingredient for vision is focus. A long and rambly vision is one you can't follow.

If you know the vision you want to chase, sharpen it by trimming it down to just six words. List them out below. If you aren't sure yet, use the examples at the bottom of this page and the questions on the next page to get the wheels turning. Then take a stab at it below.

MY VISION:

EXAMPLES:

FINISH	SCHOOL	WORK	HARD
LAND	JOB	WIN	BIG
SUPPORT	MYSELF	STAY	HUMBLE

NO	DEBT	GOOD	HUSBAND
MEANINGFUL	WORK	GOOD	DAD
BLESS	OTHERS	GOOD	FRIEND

1

*If you could be remembered for only one thing,
what would it be?*

2

What is important, but you have trouble making time for it?

3

*Twenty-five years from now, what will you wish you'd
said yes to earlier?*

CHALLENGE THREE: GHOSTS OF VISIONS PAST

In the space below, glue or duct-tape things that represent visions you once had but have given up on. When you're finished, consider the questions on the next page.

1

What did it feel like to confront visions you've given up on? Any emotions well up?

_____

2

We're not meant to chase every vision, and sometimes it's okay to give up on them. Which visions of the past are you at peace about leaving behind?

_____

3

Are there visions from the past you should re-engage? How can you do that today?

_____

CHALLENGE FOUR: A GREAT WORK

Every man of consequence is propelled forward by his vision. And every man of consequence will face haters, detractors, and naysayers.

The biblical hero Nehemiah had a vision to rebuild the protective wall around Jerusalem. For decades, it had lain in pieces, devastated by a foreign army. When the haters showed up to heckle and distract him, he yelled back:

> I am doing a great work and I cannot come down. Why should the work stop while I leave it and come down to you? (Nehemiah 6:3)

GO FIND A BRICK.
RUB IT ON THE NEXT PAGE.   – – – – – – – ➔

See the tears it creates? Vision is like that. It can feel rough to those who don't understand it. It tears less important things that get in its way. It has a weight that boys try to avoid. But like a brick, vision stands.

Vision is taking the long view, for the long haul, every day—rain or shine, believers or haters.

Write down the vision you are chasing on the brick, and set it in a place where you will see it every day. Let it serve as a reminder to not give up on your great work.

RUB BRICK ON PAGE UNTIL
THIS TYPE IS UNREADABLE

TALK
QUESTIONS FOR THE GROUP

GROUP WARMUP QUESTIONS

These are questions to unpack your MOVE challenges. Everybody gets to answer one—user's choice. One minute each, max.

VISION QUEST

Where did you toss your book? Did you learn anything about the effort vision requires?

HYPERFOCUS

Did you sharpen your vision down to a fine point? If so, share your six words with the group.

GHOSTS OF VISIONS PAST

Are there any visions you've given up on that you need to revive? How will you do that this week?

A GREAT WORK

What did you write on your brick, and what tangible steps are you taking toward that vision this week?

GROUP TALKING POINTS

This is the good stuff. Spend most of your group time here.

Do you have a long-term vision for your life? If so, what is it? If not, what are some ideas on what it could be? Workshop with the guys in this group.

Is your vision for life big enough—or have you weenied out into chasing an easy or safe dream?

Is the vision you're chasing your own, or have you (knowingly or unknowingly) adopted someone else's vision for your life?

A strong vision will dictate what you say yes and no to. Are there things you should be saying no to because they don't align with your vision? Are you saying the right yeses?

Men play the long game. What decisions are you making right now that are difficult but you expect to pay off in the long run?

Who is the last person you pissed off because of your commitment to your vision? If it hasn't happened recently, your vision probably isn't strong enough.

WRITE IT DOWN

While men default to action, it's a good idea to regularly pause, reflect, and record.

Take a few minutes to answer the questions below individually, then use your answers during the group prayer time to follow.

1

What do you think God is saying to you about vision? Be specific.

_____

2

How can you put it into action in the next seven days?

_____

CUT A COVENANT

A covenant is an ancient word for a promise. It's used throughout the Bible, especially in regard to promises made between God and man.

In the book of Job, the title character does something interesting. He makes a covenant with himself.

These five marks are like that. They are an agreement—with yourself, with your community, and with God—that you want to walk in courageous manhood.

In Hebrew, one of the ancient languages of the Bible, the verb meaning "to seal a covenant" literally translates as "to cut." Covenants weren't sealed with a handshake or a ceremony but with the spilling of an animal's blood. They were literally cut, with the death of the sacrificial animal adding substantial weight and significance to the agreement.

At the end of each mark, we'll pray together. I'll lead, but you'll be prompted to pray out loud as well. If we're going to walk in courageous manhood, we need God's help and the support of each other.

It is vital to pray for things that will make your life better. Think of this as a final act of vision—purpose that directs your steps toward a more meaningful and fulfilling life.

When we're finished, as an act of cutting this covenant with ourselves, we'll add a hash mark on the back cover of this book—using a knife, a fat Sharpie, a piece of duct tape, spray paint, or whatever we can find.

Let's get to it.

A PRAYER FOR VISION

GROUP LEADER, BEGIN THIS PRAYER EXPERIENCE WITH THE SCRIPT BELOW. WHEN YOU GET TO THE BOX, ALLOW EACH MEMBER TO SHARE THEIR PRAYER WITH THE GROUP USING THE TEMPLATE.

Father—

You are a God of vision. You have plans, aspirations, and hopes for your world. That includes every man here.

We are inspired by your vision, and we want to be men of vision. Men who are focused on the long game, willing to break through barriers to chase the things that matter.

These are the lessons we feel you teaching us, and the things you want us to do around vision:

EVERYONE IN THE GROUP, PRAY USING THIS TEMPLATE.

God, I think you are saying _____ to me about vision, and that you want me to _____.

GROUP LEADER, FINISH UP BY PRAYING THIS OVER THE GROUP.

Keep our eyes set forward, and help us push each other in the right direction.

We cut this covenant with ourselves, with your help, to be men of vision. Amen.

Now go mark the back of your book. Well done.

NOTES

MEN TAKE A MINORITY POSITION

MARK TWO

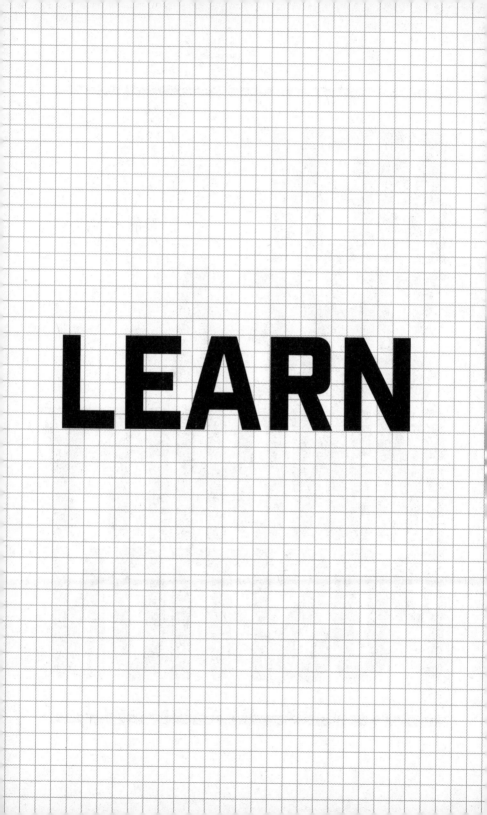

WANT TO TALK ABOUT A MINORITY POSITION? HOW ABOUT WILLINGLY CUTTING OFF THE SKIN COVERING THE TIP OF YOUR PENIS?

While you're probably wincing right now, this isn't written for shock value. Circumcision was a cornerstone act of faith in the Old Testament—and an incredibly aggressive minority position to take.

Back to our man Abraham. Vision for something better had led him to pack up everything and move to a new land.

He settles in his new hometown . . . and then waits. And waits. And waits. Over the next twenty-five years, God shows up multiple times, reminding Abraham that he will keep his promise—but from all outward appearances, it doesn't look likely. Abraham is nearing a hundred years old, with no son, no nation coming from his bloodline, and no blessing for the world.

Then, when Abraham is ninety-nine years old, God shows up again with a strange request: circumcise yourself, and every male in your household, as a sign of our covenant.

Remember, covenants were ancient promises established not with a handshake or a contract but a cut.

Incredibly, Abraham agrees to God's request. Imagine that. Now imagine explaining to every male in your large household (extended family, servants, etc.) that they're going to do the same.

Abraham doesn't just agree, he acts quickly and decisively. Genesis 17:26 says he goes to task that very day. No hesitation. No procrastination. He jumps into action, doing something few people would dare to do.

Why would he agree to this? He wants the blessings of God more than he fears the discomfort of a bad day. That's vision leading to a minority position.

A year later, when that old man finally holds his newborn son in his arms, the pain of that circumcision is miles behind him.

It's unlikely God will ask you to go chop-chop on your wee-wee, but there's a biblical truth here. Minority positions require vision. You have to see past the discomfort in order to move through the pain and into the new place beyond.

Standing up for the ridiculed employee. Being honest about the sales report. Letting your wife win the next fight. Taking time off work to spend with your kids. Not complaining about your boss. Visiting your elderly neighbor. Giving away 10 percent of your income. We're surrounded by potential minority positions, but only the men will recognize them and step into that territory—because only men are willing to stand out from the crowd.

Minority positions get the attention of others, and not always in ways you want. I can almost guarantee you will be ridiculed, be misunderstood, and suffer because of the minority positions you take. But they also get the attention of God. He looks down and sees a man willing to do the right thing, even when it's difficult. That's the kind of man he uses and blesses.

IF YOU WANT SOMETHING DIFFERENT, YOU HAVE TO DO SOMETHING DIFFERENT.

IT STARTS WITH TAKING MINORITY POSITIONS.

MOVE

PERSONAL CHALLENGES

CHALLENGE ONE: AVENGERS ASSEMBLE

Every man who lives a meaningful life will take minority positions. As we prepare to face our own, we can learn from the men of mettle who've gone before us.

This page is chock-full of minority-position-taking superheroes from history. **Read through the names and put a star beside any you recognize. Then complete the prompts below.**

Ernest Shackleton
Winston Churchill
Jackie Robinson
Frederick Douglass
Abraham Lincoln
William Wallace
John Marrant
Dietrich Bonhoeffer
Lemuel Haynes
Daniel Hale Williams

Arthur Guinness
Nelson Mandela
August Landmesser
William Wilberforce
Alan Shepard
Maximilian Kolbe
Moses
Richard Allen
William Tyndale

1

Look at the names without stars. Circle two.

2

Do a quick Wikipedia search on each name you circled. What minority positions did these men take? What aspect of their character do you most admire?

COME TO YOUR GROUP READY TO SHARE WHAT YOU'VE LEARNED.

CHALLENGE TWO: START SMALL

Taking minority positions is a muscle that needs to be built—and there's no shame in starting small.

Read through the challenges below. Each one is designed to get you reps in swimming upstream.

Put an X by two you want to try this week, and document your experiences on the next page.

☐ Pray for someone in person, out loud.

☐ For an entire day, follow every single posted speed limit sign and come to a complete stop at all stop signs.

☐ Pay for the person in line behind you.

☐ Write and send an encouraging letter (the more detailed, the better) to someone who has influenced you.

☐ Wear the rival team's jersey on game day.

☐ Stay in a public place until you feel God asking you to pray for, or help, someone you don't know. Then do it.

☐ Return every abandoned shopping cart in the store's parking lot. Yep, every single one.

DAY	MINORITY POSITION	MY REACTION
TUES.	*Prayed for a stranger in public*	*The stranger was hesitant at first, but then opened up about family stress. He seemed really grateful afterward. I realize I rarely slow down enough to hear God's promptings, and it felt great to take a risk.*

CHALLENGE THREE: CUT IT IN STONE

Taking minority positions isn't easy. It's hard work, requiring intentionality, focus, and a great deal of courage.

The most courageous people I know don't necessarily feel courageous—instead, they've anchored themselves to something much larger than they are. They can take steps forward because they're convinced they don't move alone. They cut the promises of Scripture in the stone of their mind, so that when an opportunity presents itself, they don't have to think twice about it. It's muscle memory.

On the next page are four passages from the Bible that have inspired generations of men to be bold and courageous in the face of adversity and pressure.

Choose one. Cut it out. Then tape it on your bathroom mirror or on the dash of your car where you will see it every day. Repeat it. Memorize it. Cut it into your mind. Then let it push you to make a courageous move toward minority positions.

BE WATCHFUL, STAND FIRM IN THE FAITH, ACT LIKE MEN, BE STRONG.

1 CORINTHIANS 16:13

IN THIS WORLD YOU WILL HAVE TROUBLE. BUT TAKE HEART! I HAVE OVERCOME THE WORLD.

JOHN 16:33 NIV

BE STRONG, AND SHOW YOURSELF A MAN, AND KEEP THE CHARGE OF THE LORD YOUR GOD, WALKING IN HIS WAYS.

1 KINGS 2:2-3

BE STRONG AND COURAGEOUS. DO NOT FEAR OR BE IN DREAD OF THEM, FOR IT IS THE LORD YOUR GOD WHO GOES WITH YOU. HE WILL NOT LEAVE YOU OR FORSAKE YOU.

DEUTERONOMY 31:6

CHALLENGE FOUR: RIP IT OUT

One of the most painful parts of growing into manhood is confronting the failures of boyhood. But in order to move forward, we have to deal with what lies behind.

Think of a time when you didn't take a minority position—when you knew the right thing to do but caved to the pressure to fit in. It could be something from twenty years ago or just last week—that time you overindulged and made a fool of yourself, got complacent in a relationship, or didn't stand up to your boss.

Describe the situation below, then turn to the next page.

It's time to leave this situation behind. Take a minute to honestly talk to God about it, confess your mistake, and ask for his forgiveness.

Done? Then rip this page out. God has removed this mistake from your record, so this page doesn't need to exist any longer.

Crumple up the page and get rid of it however you want—trash, recycling, fire, shredder.

YOU ARE FORGIVEN. IT'S TIME TO MOVE FORWARD.

HE DOES NOT DEAL WITH US
ACCORDING TO OUR SINS,

NOR REPAY US ACCORDING
TO OUR INIQUITIES....

AS FAR AS THE EAST IS
FROM THE WEST,

SO FAR DOES HE REMOVE OUR
TRANSGRESSIONS FROM US.

AS A FATHER SHOWS
COMPASSION TO HIS CHILDREN,

SO THE Lord SHOWS
COMPASSION TO THOSE
WHO FEAR HIM.

PSALM 103:10, 12-13

TALK

QUESTIONS FOR THE GROUP

GROUP WARMUP QUESTIONS

Everyone gets to choose one question to answer,
but keep it short and sweet.

AVENGERS ASSEMBLE

*Who did you choose? Brief your group on what you
learned.*

START SMALL

*In what ways did you swim upstream? How do you see
this building muscle for taking more "significant" minority
positions later?*

CUT IT IN STONE

*Which Scripture did you choose, and why? Now prove
you've memorized it.*

RIP IT OUT

*How comfortable are you with receiving forgiveness
from God? Is it hard to believe that your mistakes can be
forgiven?*

GROUP TALKING POINTS

This is what you came here for. Enjoy.

Describe a time recently when you took a minority position. How did it feel?

Men who take minority positions will face criticism from the majority. What is your default reaction to criticism? Does your default need to change?

Can you think of anything in your life that you've softened your position on, or even avoided altogether, to avoid criticism? What would it look like to regain a minority position?

*In **The Five Marks of a Man** I wrote about my friend Brian who hates yard work. I learned a simple equation from his crumbling foundation:*

Small weeds + Time = Big problems

Take an honest look at your life. Where are there small weeds that you've been ignoring? How can you get started on them this week?

Men are in the minority, but if they want to stand strong, they can't be isolated. Who needs your support for a minority position they are taking?

WRITE IT DOWN

Before finishing Mark II, take time to pause, reflect, and record what you've been experiencing. Do this individually, then use it to inform your group prayer experience.

1

What do you think God is saying to you about taking minority positions? Be specific.

2

How can you put that into action in the next seven days?

A PRAYER FOR TAKING MINORITY POSITIONS

GROUP LEADER, LEAD THROUGH THIS PRAYER EXPERIENCE USING THE PROMPT BELOW.

Father—

You are a bold God. You take risks. You stand up for the ignored, the forgotten, and the mistreated. You never take your cues from the crowd.

You are faithful, fearless, and strong. And we want to be like you.

We feel you pushing us to move toward this minority position:

EVERYONE IN THE GROUP PRAY, USING THIS TEMPLATE.

God, I feel you are saying _____ to me about minority positions, and that you want me to _____.

GROUP LEADER, FINISH US OUT USING THE PROMPT BELOW.

Give us boldness and strength to do the right thing even when the pressure is on.

We cut this covenant with ourselves, with your help, to be men who take minority positions. Amen.

That's another mark down.

You know the drill. As a team, add a second hash mark to the back of your book. Well done.

NOTES

MEN ARE TEAM PLAYERS

MARK THREE

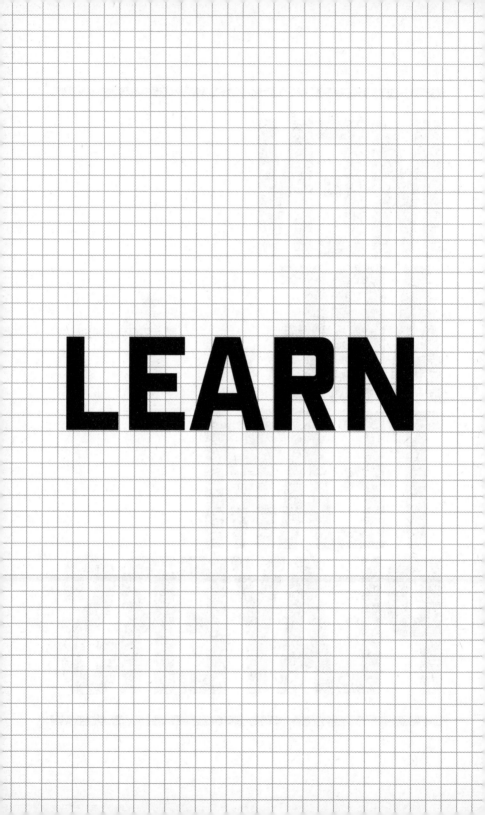

A knife has one simple purpose. Interestingly, the thing it was created to do is also what dulls it.

While the edge of a knife may look sleek, even one use creates microscopic notches on the blade. Use after use only amplifies the effect. Before long, that sleek edge looks more like a tiny mountain range. It's been dulled.

It's the same with us. The things we were created to do—work, provide, protect—can dull us. Before long, we've lost our cutting edge and aren't good for much. But just like a dulled blade can be sharpened, friendships and fun restore us.

The Bible says it this way:

> As iron sharpens iron,
>   so one person sharpens another.
>   (Proverbs 27:17 NIV)

It's been said over and over, but it bears repeating one more time: If you don't have a pack, you're dull. If you aren't having some type of regular fun with that pack, you're dull. You need other people to get your edge back.

The three processes for restoring a sharp cutting edge to a dulled blade are also the things friends do for us.

- **Sharpening** removes steel from a knife, producing a new cutting edge. Inconsistencies are smoothed out as the blade is moved against a rough surface. Good friends will do this too. They aren't afraid to have difficult conversations that will help you move into a sharper future.

- When you use your knife, debris collects on the blade. **Stropping**, moving the blade along a leather strap (like a belt), clears the debris and keeps the edge clean and sharp. This is the power of fun. It takes revenge on the stress of everyday life, clearing it away so you keep your edge.

- **Honing**, moving the blade against a piece of steel, keeps it sharp by realigning the cutting edge. Because honing restores without removing steel, it can be done daily. It's the same with friends. Their influence is a daily realignment that keeps you sharp.

That's not to say these processes are necessarily pleasant for the knife. When we intentionally put ourselves around other men, giving them an honest look into our lives, there can be friction, heat, and even sparks. But in the end, it will leave you sharper.

Have a pocketknife lying around? Dig it out and carry it around with you this week as a tangible reminder to be a team player. If it's dull, try one of the processes just described, and consider how the right team around you will do the same for your life.

Reading Scripture is an important spiritual discipline. So are prayer, tithing, and serving.

BUT IF I COULD GIVE ONE SPIRITUAL SKILL TO EVERY MAN I KNOW, IT WOULD BE GROWING LASTING FRIENDSHIPS. THEY'RE THAT VITAL.

MEN ARE TEAM PLAYERS.

MOVE

PERSONAL CHALLENGES

CHALLENGE ONE: DREAM TEAM

You can't be a team player without a team. The good news? You already exist on multiple teams. Your family, your work pod, your friend group, Saturday sports league—even the HOA—they're all teams.

While an MVP plays for personal stats, team players are focused on the team's overarching goal—they play for Super Bowl rings instead of MVP trophies.

What teams are you a part of? What are their goals? Are you playing like an MVP or a team player—and how do you know?

Fill out the scorecards for your teams, using the one below as an example.

SCORECARD	
TEAM:	*WORK*
GOAL:	*SELL AD SPACE*
(MVP) or **TEAM PLAYER**	
WHY:	*MAD THAT MY IDEA WASN'T CHOSEN*

SCORECARD

TEAM:

GOAL:

MVP or TEAM PLAYER

WHY:

SCORECARD

TEAM:

GOAL:

MVP or TEAM PLAYER

WHY:

SCORECARD

TEAM:

GOAL:

MVP or TEAM PLAYER

WHY:

SCORECARD

TEAM:

GOAL:

MVP or TEAM PLAYER

WHY:

CHALLENGE TWO: A SIMPLE PLAN

When's the last time you did something fun with someone you enjoy (and who doesn't live in your house)? If it's been more than seven days, you're in danger of burning out.

Fun isn't frivolous, and it doesn't have to be complicated. Pick something you enjoy, pair it with someone you like being around, and you're there. It really is that simple.

Below, write out names of people who come to mind. On the next page, circle ideas that sound interesting. Then, connect the two.

When you're finished, reach out to someone right away about having some fun, and record your plan in the space provided.

CLOSEST FRIEND AT WORK

LAST GUY YOU TEXTED

NEIGHBORHOOD FRIEND

LAST PERSON YOU SAID,
"WE SHOULD CATCH UP" TO

FRIEND FROM SCHOOL

OLDEST FRIEND YOU HAVE

FUN

Go for a hike	Wrench on a car	Take the motorcycles out	Go camping
Build a model train	Do a puzzle	Play chess in a park	Brew your own beer
Host a bourbon tasting party	Test-drive a fancy car	Play darts in a pub	Visit a boxing gym
Join a book club	Go to a record store	Join a sports league	Play paintball
Learn to smoke meat	Make your own hot sauce	Go hunting	Become a cigar aficionado
Start a garden	Learn to pick locks	Organize a poker game	Rehab old furniture

Write in your own idea of fun:

_____

WHO DID YOU INVITE?

WHAT WILL YOU DO?

WHEN WILL YOU DO IT?

CHALLENGE THREE: HUNTING LICENSE

Who calls you on your BS? If you don't have anyone willing to do that, you either (a) don't have real friends or (b) haven't given them access.

This challenge is about solving the second problem.

Men hear hard truths from people they trust and admire, because they have the vision that it will help make them a better husband, father, employee, and friend.

Think about your friends. Who is trustworthy? Whose opinion do you value? Who has aspects of their life worth imitating? Who answers to a higher authority and could push you to be better?

That man (or men) needs a hunting license for your life—the authority to kill anything, at any time, for your benefit.

Choosing who gets a license isn't a decision to be taken lightly. Take some time, right now, to ask God who should have a license for your life. Write any names that come to mind below.

FRIENDS

I just purchased a license and tag for hunting elk in Idaho. It wasn't cheap, and neither is the invitation to grant someone access to your life. It won't cost money, but it will cost your ego—a price we need to be willing to pay.

Look at the list you compiled. Assume that if a name came to mind, it's from God. Reach out to at least one of those men today, and ask if they're willing to carry a hunting license for your life.

If you need a script, use the one below as an example, or modify it to create your own. The language isn't the important thing, it's making the ask.

YOU ARE A FRIEND THAT I ADMIRE. I NEED A TEAM AROUND ME TO MAKE SURE I'M AT MY BEST. I TRUST YOU TO HAVE A HUNTING LICENSE TO MY LIFE. IF YOU SEE SOMETHING IN MY LIFE THAT YOU THINK NEEDS TO DIE, YOU HAVE A LICENSE TO TELL ME, ANYTIME, ANYWHERE. ARE YOU WILLING TO DO THAT FOR ME?

CHALLENGE FOUR: THE FIRE AND THE FIX

Life can be difficult. Stress, anxiety, and fear have become the norm. No one is immune to feeling the burn.

But you're not a victim. God has given you two fists to punch back at the heaviness of life—friends and fun.

With loneliness at an all-time high in our world, it's no wonder every other social ill is on the rise as well. You weren't created to be a lone wolf, and you can't thrive that way. Without a pack, and without fun, your life will burn out.

In the space below, list friends that you'd consider your pack, or men you'd like to form a pack with.

FRIENDS

On the front and back of this page, list everything in life that feels like a fire—stressors, anxieties, and fears.

In the space below, list every activity you can think of that feels like fun—things that help take the stress of life away.

FUN

Now, go grab a lighter and head outside.

Fold the book open so the stressors page is standing up. Light that page on fire and let it burn for as long as you're comfortable. That's what unchecked stress feels like.

When you're ready, close the book. The friends and fun pages will choke out and extinguish the fire. The same is true in your everyday life.

Friends and fun are the fix to life's flame. Having a pack isn't just a good idea, it's a God idea. (Check out Proverbs 17:17, 18:24, or 27:6 if you don't believe me.)

FIND GOOD MEN TO RUN WITH, AND MAKE TIME FOR FUN.

TALK

QUESTIONS FOR THE GROUP

GROUP WARMUP QUESTIONS

Everyone answer one question below in sixty seconds or less. Go.

DREAM TEAM

Which of your teams is most in need of you showing up as a team player this week?

A SIMPLE PLAN

Have you executed your fun plan? If not, why not? If so, how did it go?

HUNTING LICENSE

Who did you ask to have a hunting license for your life? How did it go?

THE FIRE AND THE FIX

What do you need to do this week to tamp back the fire of stress and anxiety?

GROUP TALKING POINTS

This is why your group is together. Major on these questions.

Have you ever had a nickname? Tell the group the story behind it.

Are you living as a lone wolf, or do you belong to a pack?

- *If you don't have a pack, what activity could you do with other guys in order to connect? Could it become a regular thing?*

- *If you do have a pack, how is it going? What are you doing to stay together and engaged?*

What is one way you can be a team player in your home this week? At work? With friends?

Describe a time when you were honest with another man about what you were truly feeling—whether it be anger, fear, sadness, excitement, or joy. Was it difficult or easy to share?

Encouragement means to put strength and courage into someone else. Who do you know that needs some of that this week, and when can you give it?

Who or what is the ultimate authority in your life, and do you regularly connect with other men who answer to that same authority?

WRITE IT DOWN

Mark Three is coming to a close. Take time to answer these questions individually.

This week, share your answers with the group before the group prayer experience, where you'll be praying for each other.

1

What do you think God is saying to you about being a team player? Be specific.

2

How can you put that into action in the next seven days?

A PRAYER FOR TEAM PLAYERS

BACK TO YOU, GROUP LEADER. TAKE YOUR TEAM THROUGH THIS PROMPT.

Father—

It is a mystery of faith, but you are also a team player. You've existed with the Son and Holy Spirit and worked as a team since before the beginning of all things.

If team is the way you choose to exist, it must be vital. We want to do the same.

As we take time to pray for each other, we thank you for this team you've put together.

EVERYONE PRAY FOR THE PERSON TO YOUR RIGHT, USING THE PROMPT BELOW AND THE ANSWERS THAT PERSON SHARED WITH THE GROUP.

Lord, I thank you for _____ . Build him up in the area of _____, where you've been speaking to him about being a team player. Pour blessings into his life as he takes action through _____ . Amen.

GROUP LEADER, WHEN EVERYONE HAS PRAYED, CLOSE OUT WITH THE WORDS BELOW.

We cut this covenant with ourselves, with your help, to be men who are team players. Amen.

Another mark bites the dust. Time to mark your progress on the back cover. Good work.

NOTES

MEN WORK

MARK FOUR

BOYS DO EVERYTHING THEY CAN TO AVOID IT, BUT THERE'S NO GETTING AROUND THIS ONE: MEN WORK. IT'S BEEN THAT WAY FROM THE VERY BEGINNING.

Before anything imperfect had entered God's world, the first man and woman were in a garden paradise called Eden. They weren't sunbathing nude and sipping mai tais. They were working.

Genesis 2:15 says God put the man in the garden to "work it and take care of it" (NIV). Sounds pretty cut-and-dried to me.

Men work because we're made of dirt.

That same chapter in Genesis says God formed the first man out of dry dust from the ground. Rather than meaning we're worthless, the fact we're made of dirt is profound.

Nothing on earth would grow—fruits, veggies, trees, and everything else that eats them—without good soil for the roots to dig into.

It's the same with us. Like good soil, we're all expected to produce. That's what sets the men apart from the boys. While the boys are consuming, getting all they can for themselves, avoiding work at all costs, men are producing for others.

Being made of dirt is also a tangible reminder that we aren't that important compared to God. Like dirt that's worked to produce a harvest, we create value through the work we do. Some of our dirt is the land we work, raising crops and livestock. Others work their dirt by making sales calls or balancing books. You might work your dirt by teaching students, buffing floors, or stocking shelves. Each role is important and the work valuable.

Jesus made this dirt connection clear in one of his most famous teachings. He compared everyone on earth to soil and God to a farmer sowing seed. Some soil was too hard to produce a crop. Other soil was so rocky the seed couldn't develop strong roots. Other soil was so covered with thorns and thistles, it choked the plant out. But there was some good soil. When the seed found it, it grew and produced a bumper crop.

Farmers can't do much to control the rain or sunshine, but they can amend their soil. Hard soil can be worked. Rocky soil can be filtered. Weedy and thorny soil can be cleared. Nutrient-deficient soil can be amended with compost and additives.

It might take work, but no soil is beyond hope. Neither are you.

The fact that you were made from dirt doesn't make you less valuable. If anything, it makes you all the more valuable. You were made to produce.

GO FIND SOME DIRT AND SMEAR IT ON THIS PAGE. CONSIDER IT A CONTRACT WITH YOURSELF AND GOD THAT YOU WILL HONOR THE CALL TO BE A MAN WHO WORKS.

MOVE

PERSONAL CHALLENGES

CHALLENGE ONE: A NEW BOSS

Whether you love your job or dread it, everything can change with a perspective tweak.

Colossians 3:23–24 says,

> *Whatever you do, work at it with all your heart, as working for the Lord, not for human masters. . . . It is the Lord Christ you are serving. (NIV)*

If you flip burgers, then you're fixing lunch for Jesus. If you crunch numbers, you're preparing Jesus's taxes. If you write or teach or sell or manufacture, you're doing it for Jesus.

Find a black Sharpie and write 3:23–24 on the inside of your wrist, where you'll see it all day. (If that's a no-go at your job, write 3:23–24 on a piece of paper and stick it in your pocket.)

Every time you see that Scripture reference, be reminded who you are serving—on the jobsite, at home, running errands, or out on the town with friends.

MEN WORK HARD TO SERVE AND EXPERIENCE GOD.

CHALLENGE TWO: CHOOSE TO LOSE

Men work . . . but what we get done is not what defines us.

Men work to experience God, not to earn his love or favor. Men work to serve others, not to prove to ourselves (or anyone else) that we're capable. Men work to produce, not to merely climb an org chart.

The Bible says you are God's son (1 John 3:1), made in his image (Genesis 1:27). God's work always benefits others. Yours should too.

Make an intentional choice to do work that won't elevate your status—do something purely out of gaining muscle in serving others.

It might be taking out the trash before you're asked, encouraging a rival at work, or helping a neighbor with a repair project.

By willingly taking the low position, you remember that success isn't everything. The world would say you are losing, but God sees that you're gaining ground.

The Bible also says that humility comes before honor (Proverbs 15:33). It's time to go get you some.

Document your losing adventure on the next page.

HOW DID YOU LOSE? _____

HOW DID IT FEEL? _____

WHAT DID YOU LEARN? _____

EXAMPLE:

Brought donuts to the office.

People were excited. That felt good.

I can do more to know my coworkers better.

EXAMPLE:

Did at least one chore every day that wasn't assigned to me.

The mood in my house is a lot lighter and people felt appreciated and seen.

Simple gestures can go a long way in relationships.

CHALLENGE THREE: EIGHT-HOUR POWER-UP

There's a secret to having better and more productive work whether you go to an office, a factory, or stay home. It's sleep. And you're probably not getting enough of it.

On average, men need at least eight hours of sleep every night to be refreshed and restored for the next day's work. Are there exceptions? Yes, but it's probably not you.

Tomorrow's work starts at bedtime today. So put your phone away. Turn the TV off. Cut the light. And sleep.

Get a solid eight hours of sleep for the next seven days. When the week is up, reflect on your attitude, work output, and energy level.

Make your plan of attack below:

TIME I GET UP:
_____

NEW BEDTIME (TO GET EIGHT HOURS):
_____

ADJUSTMENTS I NEED TO MAKE TO SUCCEED:
_____

CHALLENGE FOUR: DIRTY WORK

We've already covered how God made humanity from dirt, and that Jesus compared people to different types of soil. Time to turn the focus on yourself.

Find a Bible and read Jesus's parable of the sower for yourself. You'll find it in Matthew 13:1–9. Then, jump ahead and read his explanation of it in verses 18–23.

After you read, consider the questions below.

1

Where in your life do you feel like good soil? Where do you feel like rocky, thorny, or hard soil?

2

It's dirty work, but soil can be amended. Think about one of the places where you feel like less than good soil. What can you put into place this week to make yourself more fruitful in the future?

Now go do it. Tear out the next page, and hang it somewhere as a reminder that men produce.

A SOWER WENT OUT TO SOW. AND AS HE SOWED, SOME SEEDS ... FELL ON GOOD SOIL AND PRODUCED GRAIN, SOME A HUNDREDFOLD, SOME SIXTY, SOME THIRTY.

MATTHEW 13:3-4, 8

TALK

QUESTIONS FOR THE GROUP

GROUP WARMUP QUESTIONS

Everyone share an answer to one of the questions below. Sixty seconds on the clock per person. GO!

A NEW BOSS

How did shifting your perspective change your workday? Your attitude? Your goals or focus?

CHOOSE TO LOSE

How did you choose to lose? How did it feel and what did you learn about Scripture's promise that "humility comes before honor"?

EIGHT-HOUR POWER-UP

What was your biggest barrier to getting adequate sleep? How did having more sleep influence your week, and will you continue this moving forward?

DIRTY WORK

Where are you focusing on being more fruitful, and what are you doing to amend that "soil"?

GROUP TALKING POINTS

You know what to do by now. So get to it.

Share with the group about either your first or worst job. What lessons did you learn from it?

Do you tend to think of work as inherently good or inherently bad? Why?

Share a time when hard work grew you in a significant way. How did it do this, and how did it change your life or perspective?

Is there something you're avoiding right now because it feels like work—even though you know it's the right thing to do?

Read Colossians 3:23–24 again. If you walked into work tomorrow believing Jesus is your boss, what would look different?

Work goes well beyond just a nine-to-five job. It's an attitude of healthy aggression that's willing to sweat for what matters. In what areas of your life are you being lazy or passive right now? What would it look like to recommit to hard work?

WRITE IT DOWN

Take some individual time to reflect on this mark.
Record your answers below, then use them during the
group prayer experience.

1

What do you think God is saying to you about work?
Be specific.

2

How can you put that into action in the next seven days?

A PRAYER FOR WORKING

Father—

We're not just robots, cogs in a machine, or mindless laborers. You have created us with giftings, abilities, and aptitudes that you want to use to produce fruit.

EVERYONE IN THE GROUP, PRAY USING THIS TEMPLATE.

God, I feel you are saying _____ to me about work, and that you want me to _____ .

GROUP LEADER, FINISH USING THE PROMPT BELOW.

Whatever our hands find to work at this week, be it for a paycheck or as a volunteer, on a project around the house or wrenching on a friend's truck, help us to work at it like we're working for you. Because we are.

We cut this covenant with ourselves, with your help, to be men who work and produce. Amen.

You're coming down the pike. Before you move on, etch your progress on the back of this book.

Four marks down, one to go.

NOTES

MEN
PROTECT

MARK FIVE

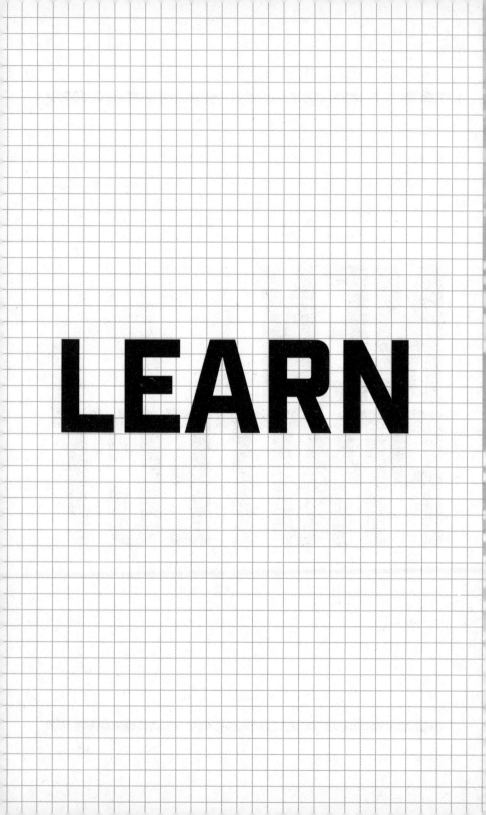

Every man I know dreams of dying courageously. We're all sure we'd take a bullet for our wife or girlfriend, lose a limb for our kids, or put it all on the line for a close friend.

But that's mostly a Hollywood daydream. Honestly, how many men do you know who've actually been shot defending their woman? I'm guessing it's a pretty low number.

In the days of knights, a shield was just as crucial a weapon as a sword. Go into battle without either and you wouldn't be around long enough to talk about it.

Men understand there may come a time to swing a sword. If someone is physically harming your wife or kids, violence may be the answer. But much more often, being a protector means being a shield.

Shields deflect harm. They stay strong after repeated attacks. They repel danger, death, and destruction. And they take massive cuts in the process.

MEN ARE ACTING AS PROTECTORS WHEN THEY LOSE IN ORDER FOR SOMEONE ELSE TO WIN.

That is the kind of self-sacrificing love modeled in the Bible.

Jesus told his followers that there was no greater love than to give up your life for your friends (John 15:13). Paul taught husbands to love their wives in the same way Christ loved the church (Ephesians 5:25).

In both examples, the baseline for love is dying.

We can say we'd take a bullet for our significant other, but I'm not sure we would unless we're already taking cuts on the small things. When was the last time you purposefully let her win a fight, listened without interrupting, or took out the trash before it spilled onto the floor? You can fight for her by being patient with her or saying yes to what she wants to do for the night.

We think we'd do anything for our kids, but I'm not sure we would if we're not already clearing our calendars to make room for their volleyball games, including them on important family decisions, or having protector conversations with their prom dates. We fight for them by helping them thrive, teaching lessons they'll never find (or even think to look for) on YouTube.

When it comes down to it, men can be swords. But in the day-to-day, they're also making intentional decisions to become shields.

**TAKE THE CUTS.
GET UNCOMFORTABLE.
CHOOSE TO LOSE.
THAT'S WHAT MEN DO,
BECAUSE MEN ARE BORN
TO BE PROTECTORS.**

MOVE

PERSONAL CHALLENGES

WHAT KIND OF PROTECTOR?

If you're a man, you're a protector. What kind? That's what we're about to find out.

Read each statement and put an X by the ones you identify with. Go with your gut. Your first answer is probably the right one.

☐ *When my friends have something to move, especially something heavy, I'm their go-to guy.* ♣

☐ *People often seek out my wisdom on major life decisions.* ♥

☐ *When there's a happy hour after work, I'm there to connect with others, even if I don't drink.* ♠

☐ *When I know a friend is having a hard time, my first thought is to Venmo them or send them a gift card.* ♦

☐ *I can sometimes overspiritualize problems or things in my life.* ♥

☐ *I often care too much about what people think of me.* ♠

☐ *Among my friends, I'm the one always getting asked to support kids' fundraisers.* ♦

- [ ] When a friend is in crisis, I am likely to arrange a Meal Train so they don't have to worry about food. ♣

- [ ] When a friend is hurting, I start a text thread to get others praying for them. ♥

- [ ] After a tough day, grabbing a drink with a friend helps me feel better. ♠

- [ ] It's easier to give money than my time. ♦

- [ ] I've been known to pass on a good book that can help a friend with something in their life. ♥

- [ ] I can sometimes be out of touch with emotions or sentimentality. ♣

- [ ] I feel more secure when I save before I spend on fun. ♦

- [ ] My social media feed is full of relationship experts, Enneagram coaches, and Brené Brown. ♠

- [ ] Surprising my significant other with tickets to the Broadway show she's been dying to see would bring me life. ♠

- [ ] I actually know what The Motley Fool is and follow @WarrenBuffetQuotes on Instagram. ♦

- [ ] When my family's car needs maintenance, it's my top priority. ♣

- [ ] On movie night, I'm choosing something like Rambo or Taken. ♣

- [ ] My favorite movies, TV shows, and books are ones where I've mined out a deeper spiritual meaning or truth. ♥

Now flip to the next page.

Each statement on the previous page was assigned a suit. **Look back at the statements you put an X beside, and tally up your totals for each suit.**

SUIT	TOTAL
♣	
♥	
♠	
♦	

Have the most ♣s? You're probably a **physical protector**. You're more likely to defend yourself and others, and to be ready to meet their tangible needs.

Have more ♥s than anything else? You're looking like a **spiritual protector**. You can see the need to come under God's protection, and you seek to bring others with you.

Have the most ♠s? You're likely a **relational protector**. You probably have many friends, enjoy spending time with them, and understand that connectedness matters.

Is ♦ your highest? You're probably a **financial protector**. You might enjoy helping others feel more secure by meeting monetary needs or funding initiatives.

1

What kind of protector are you? Do you agree?

It's great to celebrate the ways you're already protecting others. But this experience is all about growing in the five marks—if you're already good at something, there isn't much growth opportunity.

Over the next few pages, you'll find challenges grouped according to these four types of protectors. Find the page that corresponds to your lowest protector score and choose one (or both) of the challenges to help you grow in that area.

Being a complete protector means embracing each of these four areas.

PHYSICAL PROTECTOR ♣

PRACTICE PUNCHES

Even if the day-to-day life of a protector doesn't involve throwing a punch, it doesn't mean you shouldn't know how. Pull out your phone and search YouTube for "How to Throw a Punch in a Fight" (Tony Jeffries). Practice the proper form for throwing a punch. Get someone to hold the book open for you, and take aim at the bullseye on the facing page.

ACT FAST

What's the job that needs to get done but that everyone avoids? Do it today. Whether it's cleaning out the fridge in the break room or doing the mountain of laundry at home, show yourself a protector by taking action today.

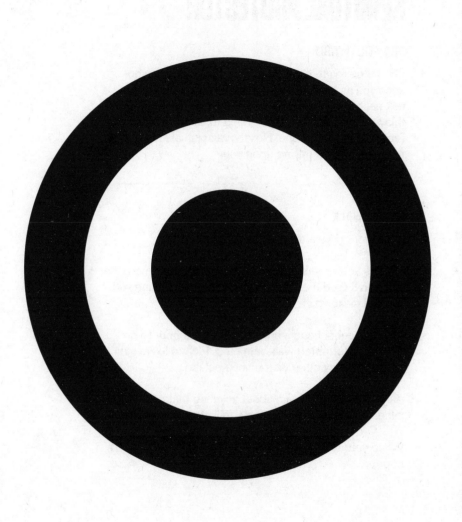

SPIRITUAL PROTECTOR ♥

PRAY OUTWARD

On the opposite page, make a list of everyone who sees you as their protector. Take time to personally ask each person how you can be praying for them this week—then do it. If you need to, set a daily alarm reminder in your phone. Flex those spiritual muscles for the people most relying upon you.

TAKE A WALK

Protectors create other protectors.

In ways you've recognized, and probably even more that you don't, God has protected you. Spending time with him will make you a better protector.

Look at your schedule and carve out one hour to go on an uninterrupted walk with God. Plan to leave your phone and any other distractions behind.

As you walk, talk to him about anything that enters your mind, and be sure to save time to listen as well.

When your time is up, write any reflections on the next page.

RELATIONAL PROTECTOR

GIVE IT AWAY, GIVE IT AWAY, GIVE IT AWAY NOW

The average person spends over three hours every day on their phone.[4] What if you could get thirty minutes of that scroll time back? Who would you give it to?

Choose a thirty-minute block three times this week and put your phone away. Hide it in a drawer, leave it in the car, or stuff it under your pillow.

Then give your thirty minutes away—play a game with your kids, grab a meal with a friend, listen to your wife without Instagram in the background.

Track your progress on the opposite page.

MENTOR MEET-UP

Luke had Obi-Wan. Daniel had Mr. Miyagi. The T. C. Williams High School football team had Coach Boone. The presence of a mentor will elevate your life.

Take stock of your relationships. Where do you see an older man whose wisdom you could benefit from?

Make the first move. Ask if you can take him to lunch or buy him a beer. If it's a good fit, ask him if you can set up a recurring time to meet.

Want to make his day? Use the word *mentor*. Every man wants to be one, but almost no one is asking.

	WHO DID I GIVE MY TIME TO?	WHAT DID WE DO?	HOW DID IT FEEL?
EXAMPLE	*My mom*	*After work I stopped by my mom's house to visit and I left my phone in the car.*	*She was initially shocked that I stopped just to check on her. But she clearly enjoyed our time together and it passed faster than I expected it to.*
DAY 1			
DAY 2			
DAY 3			

FINANCIAL PROTECTOR ◆

TRACK IT

Instead of guessing where your money goes, take one week to track every purchase. That might mean saving all your receipts or logging in to your bank app each night. Note how much you spent, where you spent it, and what you purchased. Use space on the next page or open up a fresh Google spreadsheet to make notes.

At the end of the week, look at the data you collected. Does anything stand out? For another perspective, let someone you respect (and who is good with money) look at your spending and offer coaching as well.

SPEND OR SAVE

When it comes to money, there are only two types of people: spenders and savers. Which one are you?

This week, find ways to do the opposite. If you're a natural saver, splurge on flowers for your spouse, pick up the tab at lunch, or buy a stranger's groceries. If you're a spender, cut out the daily Starbucks run or pizza night and bank that money.

Flex those financial protector muscles.

TALK

QUESTIONS FOR THE GROUP

GROUP WARMUP QUESTIONS

Choose the section that applies to you, then answer one question, ASAP.

♣ PHYSICAL PROTECTOR CHALLENGES

Practice Punch: Did you actually practice throwing a punch? Did anything feel different?

Act Fast: What job did you do? How did it feel to serve others?

♥ SPIRITUAL PROTECTOR CHALLENGES

Pray Outward: Do you have a regular rhythm of praying for others? If so, how often do you ask them what you can be praying for?

Take a Walk: What was the most difficult part of your walk? Did you feel like you heard from God?

♠ RELATIONAL PROTECTOR CHALLENGES

Give It Away: Who did you give your time to? Why did you choose them?

Mentor Meet-Up: Who did you ask, and what about them are you drawn to?

♦ FINANCIAL PROTECTOR CHALLENGES

Track It: Any surprises or learnings from your tracking exercise? Did someone else examine it?

Spend or Save: Are you a saver or a spender, and how did you flex a different muscle this week?

GROUP TALKING POINTS

Last group discussion. Chop-chop.

When you think about protectors in your life, who comes to mind? How did they protect you, and how did that form you?

Can you think of a time when you stepped in to protect someone else? How about a time when you failed to do so, even though you knew it was the right thing to do?

Think back to the protector assessment. What type of protector role do you naturally default to? What evidence from your life supports that answer?

Which is your weakest area as a protector—physical, spiritual, relational, or financial? How did the challenges in that area push you?

As a protector, are you more comfortable being a sword or a shield? How might God be pushing you more in the other direction?

When you are around, do others feel protected? Why or why not?

WRITE IT DOWN

Our last mark. Take individual time to record your answers, then use them during your final group prayer experience.

1

What do you think God is saying to you about being a protector? Be specific.

_____

2

How can you put that into action in the next seven days?

_____

A PRAYER FOR PROTECTORS

GROUP LEADER, YOU'RE UP. LEAD US THROUGH THE FINAL PRAYER
EXPERIENCE.

Father—

*You are a good protector. The Psalms describe you as a
shield, a strong tower, and our strength. You have been all
these things for us, both in ways that we recognize and in
many more that we don't.*

*We want to emulate your faithfulness and protection for
those who are depending on us.*

EVERYONE IN THE GROUP, PRAY USING THIS TEMPLATE.

*God, I feel you are saying _____ to me about being
a protector and that you want me to _____.*

GROUP LEADER, TAKE US HOME.

*Help us to be both trustworthy shields and wise swords.
Put to death any boyish predator ways that are still within
us.*

*We cut this covenant with ourselves, with your help, to be
men who are protectors. Amen.*

That's the fifth and final mark. As a group, make that final
hash mark on the back of this book. You've earned it.

A FINAL THOUGHT

You've made it to the end. Well done.

This tactical and practical guide to courageous manhood was designed to make the five marks tangible. It was created to push you into action. No one becomes a man by sitting in a circle and talking. Men act. That's what you've done.

Whether you do a formal initiation ceremony (more on that in Appendix 1) or not, hear me clearly: by completing this study, you have proven yourself a man.

You had vision to push yourself, and you did.

You took uncomfortable minority positions.

You moved through this with others, like a team player.

You worked hard and practiced being a protector.

I believe you are a man. The men who moved through this process with you believe you're a man. Now, you must believe it.

In the Bible, it says this:

> As [a man] thinketh in his heart, so is he.
> (Proverbs 23:7 KJV)

On the surface, it sounds like a pile of self-help BS, but it's true. Your thoughts influence outcomes.

If you expect to get into a fight with your spouse after work, you'll go home defensive and trigger-happy, and it'll happen.

If you are addressing the golf ball and think you will have a bad shot, a shank is just a swing away.

If you expect to have a bad day at work, even before you arrive, you'll begin to dread the day and find plenty of reasons to be let down.

If you expect time with a friend to be uplifting, more often than not, you'll go into the conversation with a light demeanor and leave it feeling better than before.

What initiation rites did for the men of old was convince them they were no longer boys. Because they walked a difficult road, came out the other side, and were acknowledged as men by senior members of their community, a switch flipped in their brains. They stopped thinking of themselves as boys. From that point on, they were men.

It was a victory that started in their minds. The final step in courageous manhood is flipping that switch in your own mind as well.

An initiation ceremony can go a long way toward achieving this. No matter how old you are, there's something powerful about a spiritually potent man declaring that you have moved into manhood.

This is what King David did while lying on his deathbed. He called his son Solomon to his side and spoke these words over the soon-to-be king:

> Be strong, act like a man, and observe what the LORD your God requires: Walk in obedience to him. . . . Do this so that you may prosper in all you do and wherever you go. (1 Kings 2:2–3 NIV)

Be strong. Follow God. Act like a man.

When you make a mistake, act like a man.
When you get a big win, act like a man.
When you are on your first date, act like a man.
When you're in a fight with your kids, act like a man.
When your spouse is hurting, act like a man.
When your friend is in need, act like a man.
When you're facing a difficult choice, act like a man.

The only way to act like a man? Think like one.

You have vision for the long game.
You take minority positions that go against the culture.
You are a team player focused on winning with others.
You work hard.
You are a protector who can be counted on.

Even when you don't feel like it.
Even when you mess up.
Even when you're stringing together some impressive losses.

You are in the upper 1 percent of all men on the planet, because you've moved through this process.

I am proud of the man you are. Keep winning the victory in your mind, and your hands and feet will follow.

No matter what tomorrow brings, you are equipped and ready to face it because you are a man.

BE STRONG.
FOLLOW GOD.
ACT LIKE A MAN.

The world needs us now more than ever.

APPENDIXES

APPENDIX 1
PLANNING YOUR INITIATION CEREMONY

Big moments in life get marked with ceremonies—graduations, weddings, baptisms. This is no different.

What you do for your initiation ceremony is up to you. But if you want some help, consider these options:

GO SOMEPLACE WILD

There's something special about putting yourself back into wild and untamed places. Pick a spot in the woods, an isolated cabin, or at least someplace away from your normal routine.

GO WITH YOUR TEAM

You didn't move into manhood isolated, and you shouldn't mark the moment alone either. Bring the guys you did this workbook with, and also consider inviting some older, wiser men to join you.

GIVE AND RECEIVE

Take time to encourage each man present with the ways you see them living into the marks. Then, have a senior member of your crew declare, "You are a man" over each person present. It isn't a bad idea to do something physical to mark the moment. Maybe a firm punch to the chest while locking eyes and giving verbal affirmation.

PRAY AND COMMIT

You can't do it all on your own power. Finish by praying for each man, asking God to cement their new position and mindset as a man.

APPENDIX 2
HOSTING A DUDE GROUP FOR THE FIRST TIME

Team is integral to manhood—but hosting a group might not be intuitive. If you're stressed about it, let these best practices put your mind at ease.

PICK YOUR TRIBE

Choose men you want to go on this journey with. They should be men who will push you, encourage you, and be committed. Variety in age, experience, and background is always a positive.

PICK YOUR TIME AND PLACE

Choose a time and place to meet regularly—a pub or basement, coffee shop or living room. It just needs to be inviting and have room for everyone.

SET THE EXPECTATION

Small talk is okay, but agree to prioritize the reason you're together: progressing through these challenges and real talk about life, family, and God.

SUPPORT EACH OTHER

That might mean something different for every dude. At minimum, it means keeping private talk private, encouraging each other's progress, and praying for each other.

NOTES

1. "Life Expectancy in the U.S. Dropped for the Second Year in a Row in 2021," Centers for Disease Control and Prevention, August 31, 2022, https://www.cdc.gov/nchs/pressroom/nchs_press_releases/2022/20220831.htm.

2. "Suicide," Mental Health Information, National Institute of Mental Health, June 2022, https://www.nimh.nih.gov/health/statistics/suicide.

3. "Excessive Alcohol Use Is a Risk to Men's Health," Centers for Disease Control and Prevention, June 2022, https://www.cdc.gov/alcohol/fact-sheets/mens-health.htm.

4. Josh Howarth, "Time Spent Using Smartphones (2023 Statistics)," Exploding Topics, January 9, 2023, https://explodingtopics.com/blog/smartphone-usage-stats.

KEEP MOVING

WEEKLY

For fresh inspiration to keep taking new ground, subscribe to *The Aggressive Life with Brian Tome* podcast, available on all major platforms.

ANNUALLY

Join Brian for **MAN CAMP**, an off-the-grid weekend created to connect you with a band of brothers reclaiming authentic manhood. It's a great opportunity to reconnect with the group you finished this guide with. Find more at ManCamp.us.

BRIANTOME.COM